Visual Geography Series®

BELGIUM

...in Pictures

Prepared by
Geography Department

Lerner Publications Company
Minneapolis

Courtesy of Belgian National Tourist Office, New York

Belgium has one of Europe's best railway networks.

This book is an all-new edition in the Visual Geography Series. Previous editions were published by Sterling Publishing Company, New York City. The text, set in 10/12 Century Textbook, is fully revised and updated, and new photographs, maps, charts, and captions have been added.

LIBRARY OF CONGRESS CATALOGING-IN-PUBLICATION DATA

Belgium in pictures / prepared by Geography Department.
    p. cm. — (Visual geography series)
    Rev. ed. of Belgium and Luxembourg in pictures / by E. W. Egan.
    Includes index.
    Summary: Describes the topography, history, society, economy, and governmental structure of Belgium.
    ISBN 0-8225-1889-9 (lib. bdg.)
    1. Belgium. [1. Belgium.] I. Egan. E. W. Belgium and Luxembourg in pictures. II. Lerner Publications Company. Geography Dept. III. Series: Visual geography series (Minneapolis, Minn.)
DH418.B444   1991
949.3—dc20
                          91-15011
                              CIP
                               AC

International Standard Book Number: 0-8225-1889-9
Library of Congress Catalog Card Number: 91-15011

VISUAL GEOGRAPHY SERIES®

Publisher
Harry Jonas Lerner
Associate Publisher
Nancy M. Campbell
Senior Editor
Mary M. Rodgers
Editors
Gretchen Bratvold
Tom Streissguth
Photo Researcher
Kerstin Coyle
Editorial/Photo Assistants
Marybeth Campbell
Colleen Sexton
Consultants/Contributors
Herman van der Wusten
Phyllis Schuster
Sandra K. Davis
Designer
Jim Simondet
Cartographer
Carol F. Barrett
Indexers
Kristine S. Schubert
Sylvia Timian
Production Manager
Gary J. Hansen

Courtesy of Belgian National Tourist Office, New York

In the lowlands of western Belgium, young cyclists enjoy touring the countryside.

Acknowledgments

Title page photo © Jerg Kroener.

Elevation contours adapted from *The Times Atlas of the World*, seventh comprehensive edition (New York: Times Books, 1985).

1 2 3 4 5 6 7 8 9 10 00 99 98 97 96 95 94 93 92 91

Photo by INBEL-Brussels

A monument in the province of East Flanders honors two Flemish painters, the brothers Jan and Hubert van Eyck. Few works by Hubert have survived, but Jan enjoyed a successful career as a court painter to Philip the Good, duke of Burgundy, in the early 1400s.

Contents

NORTH SEA

NETHERLANDS

Rhine R.

Maas R.

East Schelde

West Schelde

Zeebrugge

ANTWERP

Oostende

Damme

Brugge

EAST FLANDERS

Antwerp

ALBERT CANAL

LIMBURG

Canal

GERMANY

WEST FLANDERS

Wingene

Ghent

Dijle R.

Demer R.

Poelkapelle

Leie R.

Dendermonde

Ieper

Schelde R.

BRUSSELS

Louvain

Liège

Eupen

Senne R.

Waterloo

BRABANT

Ath

Tournai

HAINAUT

Mons

Sambre R.

Charleroi

Namur

Meuse R.

LIÈGE

Malmédy

Stavelot

St. Vith

NAMUR

LUXEMBOURG

FRANCE

Semois R.

Bastogne

LUXEMBOURG

Arlon

Virton

BELGIUM

N

↑

- - - Province Boundaries

——— Major Roads

| 0 | 30 Miles |
| 0 | 30 Kilometers |

EUROPE

BELGIUM

| 0 | 400 Miles |
| 0 | 400 Kilometers |

Arctic Circle

NORWEGIAN SEA

20°

0°

20°

60°

NORTH ATLANTIC OCEAN

20°

40°

MEDITERRANEAN SEA

40°

METRIC CONVERSION CHART
To Find Approximate Equivalents

WHEN YOU KNOW:	MULTIPLY BY:	TO FIND:
AREA		
acres	0.41	hectares
square miles	2.59	square kilometers
CAPACITY		
gallons	3.79	liters
LENGTH		
feet	30.48	centimeters
yards	0.91	meters
miles	1.61	kilometers
MASS (weight)		
pounds	0.45	kilograms
tons	0.91	metric tons
VOLUME		
cubic yards	0.77	cubic meters
TEMPERATURE		
degrees Fahrenheit	0.56 (*after* subtracting 32)	degrees Celsius

A pink moon rises over the cathedral towers of Tournai, an ancient city in Wallonia – the French-speaking region of Belgium.

Introduction

Belgium, named after early Celtic settlers called the Belgae, is a low-lying country in western Europe between the much larger nations of Germany and France. Belgium's terrain and location have made the country easy for foreigners to invade. After about 50 B.C., parts of Belgium were successively conquered by Roman, Frankish, Spanish, Austrian, French, and Dutch powers. In the twentieth century, during World Wars I and II, German forces attacked and occupied Belgium.

In spite of long periods of foreign rule, Belgians have retained a strong pride in their own history and cultural identity. Most of the people are loyal to one of

5

several local cultures, which thrive mainly in the country's two principal regions—Flanders and Wallonia.

Language divisions distinguish these regions. In Flanders, which covers northern and western Belgium, are the Flemings, who speak the Flemish dialect of Dutch. Many Flemings also know French. The French-speaking Walloons live in Wallonia, which lies in southern Belgium. Some Walloons can speak Flemish, too. In addition to language differences, Belgians also maintain ties either to the Roman Catholic religion, which strongly influences political parties, or to nonreligious political parties.

Despite these internal divisions, modern Belgium has been a leader in pursuing economic union in Europe. One of the main organizations that symbolizes such cooperation is the European Community (EC), whose policy-making headquarters is in the capital city of Brussels. As an EC member, Belgium has access to a large market and gets a share of EC investment funds. These benefits have helped Belgians to attain a high standard of living.

Courtesy of Kunsthistorischen Museums, Wien

A detail from the painting *Children's Games* by the Flemish artist Pieter Brueghel illustrates how young Belgians had fun in the 1500s.

Courtesy of Belgian Tourist Office

Decisions that govern the European Community (EC) are made at its headquarters in Brussels, the capital of Belgium. The EC pursues trade and investment policies that benefit all the members, including Belgium.

Piles of grain await collection on a farm in the Ardennes of southeastern Belgium. Although a heavily forested region, the Ardennes also supports pasture and crop farming.

1) The Land

A small, heavily urbanized country in western Europe, Belgium has only one natural boundary—the North Sea. An arm of the Atlantic Ocean, the North Sea touches Belgium's western coast. The Netherlands lies to the north, and eastern Belgium borders Germany and Luxembourg. Southern Belgium shares a long boundary with France. With 11,799 square miles of territory, Belgium is about the size of the state of Maryland.

Topography

Belgium has three principal geographic areas—the coastal and inland lowlands, the Central Plateaus, and the Ardennes. These landscape regions gradually rise in elevation. The lowlands stretch across Flanders in western and northern Belgium. The Central Plateaus extend roughly from Brussels, in central Belgium, southward to the Sambre and Meuse rivers. The forested Ardennes covers the southeastern third of the country that is part of Wallonia.

The lowlands begin at the white beaches and low sand dunes that line the North Sea. The dunes keep the sea from flooding the land during high tides. Behind the dunes are polders—low-lying lands that farmers have protected by building earthen

7

walls called dikes. Brugge, one of the oldest cities in Flanders, lies on a polder. To keep the polders dry, windmills pump out surplus water that gathers during rainstorms. Farmers in the lowlands plant crops and raise livestock on the fertile clay soil.

About 10 miles inland, the lowlands gently rise to elevations of 70 to 160 feet above sea level. Intensely farmed, this region gets its water from the Leie, Schelde,

and Demer rivers. Ghent, a major Flemish city, is a center of agriculture and textile production. The lowlands continue northward into Kempenland (or Campine), an area of marshlands and wooded hills. Within Kempenland is Antwerp, a key European port and industrial hub.

The cities of Brussels and Liège are the largest urban areas of the Central Plateaus. Several rivers cut through the region's rolling hills and wide valleys,

A Belgian rider guides his mount through the sand dunes that border the western coast.

where farmers grow grain in the rich soil. Small towns dot the land, which lies between 160 and 650 feet in altitude.

A valley formed by the Sambre and Meuse rivers separates the Central Plateaus from the Ardennes. The forests of the Ardennes cover a hilly, limestone plateau that averages 1,000 feet above sea level. In some places, elevations exceed 2,000 feet. The highest point in Belgium—Botrange Mountain—rises to 2,277 feet near the German border. Sparsely populated, the Ardennes contains many small villages.

Rivers and Canals

Because of their slow currents, Belgium's rivers are easily navigable and have been important commercial routes for centuries. The country's principal rivers are the Schelde, the Meuse, and the Sambre.

At Namur, a Wallonian city in central Belgium, the Meuse and Sambre rivers join. Bridges cross the Meuse, connecting the left and right banks of this well-preserved urban area.

Boats line the docks at Antwerp, the sprawling Belgian port on the Schelde River.

A barge motors up the Albert Canal—an 80-mile-long artificial waterway that begins in the city of Liège and curves north-westward to reach Antwerp.

The 270-mile-long Schelde begins in France and flows northward through the fertile fields of the Central Plateaus. North of Antwerp, the river crosses into the Netherlands, where a narrow strip of ter- ritory separates the Schelde into eastern and western branches. A dike has partly closed off the East Schelde from the North Sea. The West Schelde eventually widens into an estuary, where the river meets the sea. Thus, although the Schelde runs through Belgium, its sea outlet—the West Schelde—is under Dutch (Netherlandish) control.

The Meuse, a 580-mile waterway that also starts in France, winds northward into Belgium south of the city of Namur. The river crosses Belgium and flows into the Netherlands, where the Meuse becomes the Maas River. It then turns westward and feeds into the North Sea. The Sambre also originates in France and enters Belgium midway along the Belgian-French border. After traveling through the city of Charleroi, the Sambre joins the Meuse at Namur.

Belgium's extensive canal system links its rivers and eases inland transportation. Much of Antwerp's cargo arrives by way of Belgian canals. The country's longest artificial waterway—the 80-mile Albert Canal—spans the sandy marshlands of Kempenland to connect Antwerp with Liège, which lies on the Meuse. This river ties Belgium into the extensive Dutch network of waterways, which handles much of the river traffic of western Europe.

Flora and Fauna

Forests of deciduous (leaf-shedding) trees cover about one-fifth of Belgium. Kempenland and the Ardennes are the most densely wooded regions in the country. Once blanketed with birch, Kempenland has been replanted with pines that loggers cut for commercial timber and pulp. Hardwoods and evergreens grow side by side in the Ardennes, 70 percent of which is forested.

Independent Picture Service

Dense woodlands are common in southeastern Belgium, where the course of the Semois River has nearly isolated a small tree-covered piece of land.

Oak and birch are the most common native trees in Belgium, but beech and elm also thrive in the country's soil. Farmers have planted rows of poplars to serve as windbreaks between the low-lying polders. Smaller flowering plants include hyacinth, goldenrod, periwinkle, and foxglove.

Human settlement and hunting have greatly reduced the country's animal population. Boars and deer, however, still inhabit the thick forests of the Ardennes. Foxes, badgers, weasels, and hedgehogs live throughout rural Belgium. Pheasant and partridge are game birds that have survived in the nation's woodlands. Belgian fishing crews haul in herring, shrimp, and sole from the North Sea. The Meuse and other rivers provide trout and crayfish.

Climate

Like the rest of northwestern Europe, Belgium has a generally mild climate without great extremes of heat or cold. The rapid movement of air masses that blow in from the Atlantic Ocean strongly affects the weather. The winds bring heavy

Colorful screens provide privacy along the beaches of western Belgium, which attract sunbathers and swimmers in the summer months.

and frequent rainfall, which totals between 30 and 40 inches annually. The Ardennes gets some of this precipitation as snow. The air masses can also cause heavy storms to pound the Belgian coast.

The climate is milder in the low-lying regions of western Belgium than it is in the hilly Ardennes, where winters are cold and summers are warm. The country's northern and central sections have cool summers and damp, mild winters.

Temperatures in Oostende, a resort and port on the North Sea, drop to about 37° F in January, the coldest month. In July, the hottest month, Oostende's figures hover around 61° F. In Brussels, temperatures rarely fall below 36° F in January or rise above 62° F in July. Virton, a town in the southern Ardennes, has experienced lows of 0° F and highs of 97° F. Virton's averages, however, are 33° F in January and 61° F in July.

Cities

Ninety-five percent of Belgium's 9.9 million people live in urban areas. This per-

Most of the subway stops in Brussels are decorated with some form of modern art. At the Hankar Station, the artist Roger Somville applied acrylic paints to concrete to create *Notre Temps* (Our Time), a vibrant statement about humanity's march toward social justice.

On the Grand Place—a large, ornate square in central Brussels—a horse and carriage thread their way through a throng of people.

centage is the highest in Europe. The country's two main population centers are Brussels and Antwerp. Other Belgian city dwellers live in regional hubs, such as Charleroi and Liège, and in historic cities, including Ghent and Brugge.

BRUSSELS AND ANTWERP

The home of 1.1 million people, Brussels and its suburbs cover nearly half of the province of Brabant. Lying along the Senne River, Brussels has long been a meeting place for the Flemish and Walloon cultures. In modern times, the city has also become a center for international business and politics. One out of every three residents of Brussels is non-Belgian. Two languages—Flemish and French—are officially recognized, but English, German,

An officially bilingual (two-language) city, crowded Brussels has more than a million residents. Most of the people speak French, but Flemish is also used.

Central Brussels is a mixture of buildings and squares connected by a network of twisting streets. The Grand Place *(center)* is lined with a Gothic town hall, an ancient guild (trade) hall, and other original or restored structures.

and other tongues are commonly heard in the city's streets, restaurants, and parks.

Belgium's capital since 1830, Brussels is also the hub of the nation's commerce, industry, and intellectual life. Many of the city's residents, most of whom speak French, work for the national government or for international agencies headquartered in Brussels. Among the capital's leading products are textiles, chemicals, electrical equipment, machinery, and beer.

Antwerp (population 500,000), one of Europe's busiest ports, sprawls along the Schelde River. In the 1400s and 1500s, Antwerp was a prosperous trading center that attracted merchants, artists, and craftspeople. Modern Antwerp still relies on trade for income but also has petroleum

refineries, chemical firms, metal-making industries, food-processing plants, and electronics factories. For centuries, the city's diamond cutters have ranked among the best in the world, and the diamond industry continues to be important to Antwerp's economy.

SECONDARY CITIES

Charleroi, an urban area with more than 250,000 people, lies amid fertile farmland in the Sambre River Valley. Nearby coal deposits helped the city's industries to prosper in the 1800s, bringing wealth and jobs to much of Wallonia. The city's canals are lined with warehouses that once bustled with activity. Many of the metalworking forges and factories are outdated, but

The port of Antwerp handles much of the cargo that travels into and out of Belgium. Most of the traffic arrives via canals, but the city is also linked to the West Schelde — a Dutch-owned sea-lane that gives Antwerp access to the North Sea.

Charleroi is attempting to attract high-technology companies to bolster its economy.

Ghent, an old university town of 235,000 people, is the capital of the province of East Flanders. Sitting on dozens of islands at the junction of the Leie and Schelde rivers, Ghent is Belgium's second largest port.

In 1886 engineers completed a canal that links the city directly to the Schelde estuaries on the North Sea.

For centuries, Ghent has been a hub of Belgium's textile industry. In modern times, steel production and flower-growing businesses have also become important to the local economy. Ghent's architectural

Ghent had many of the traits of an industrialized city long before the machine age. In the 1200s, Ghent's guilds employed thousands of people to weave woolen cloth. Local leaders banded together to protect the cloth industry and to improve working conditions for laborers.

An arched bridge crosses a canal in Brugge, an old trading city in the province of West Flanders.

during the world wars, destroying some of its manufacturing plants. Since the post-war period, Liège has become one of Belgium's cultural centers, with cafes, cabarets, concert halls, and ballets.

Founded in the A.D. 600s, Brugge (population 120,000) flourished from the 1200s to the 1400s, when it was a member of the Hanseatic League of wealthy merchant cities. A canal connects Brugge, the capital of the province of West Flanders, to the North Sea port of Zeebrugge. Numerous bridges span Brugge's canals, which are lined with homes dating from the thirteenth century. Gothic cathedrals, broad squares, and well-preserved commercial buildings reflect the city's past as a prosperous trading center.

treasures survived occupation by German forces in World War I (1914–1918) and World War II (1939–1945). The city's ninth-century castle and its sixteenth-century town hall still stand.

Liège (population 215,000) sits on both banks of the Meuse River in eastern Belgium. The age-old administrative and commercial capital of Wallonia, the city has many hidden courtyards, narrow lanes, and steep streets. In the 1460s, Liège was leveled by Charles the Bold, a powerful duke who felt the city's people had criticized him. As a result, many of Liège's buildings date from the sixteenth century.

Using nearby supplies of minerals, Liège developed into a major manufacturer of guns and glassware in the 1800s and early 1900s. Foreign armies overran the city

Brugge's thirteenth-century belfry dominates the market square, whose buildings reflect the city's colorful history as an important commercial center.

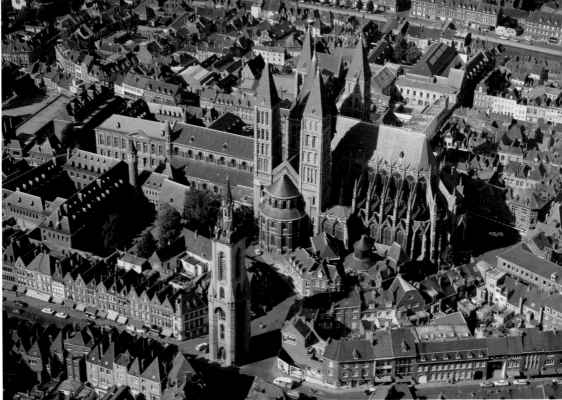

The history of Tournai spans much of the history of Belgium. The city began as a Roman settlement in the first century B.C. It later was the seat of power of Childeric, an early king of the invading Franks. Tournai's massive twelfth-century cathedral combines Romanesque and Gothic building styles. The ancient church survived French occupation in the 1300s, Protestant riots in the 1500s, and German bombs in the 1900s.

2) History and Government

Archaeologists have found the ruins of several prehistoric cultures in what is now Belgium. The remains suggest that most of the country's early inhabitants were farmers and herders. By about 3000 B.C., invasions and migrations from the east and north had changed the lifestyle of Belgium's people. Some of the newcomers were skilled metalworkers. Later arrivals introduced the practice of burning their dead and then placing the ashes in urns. These settlers, called Celts, originated in northern Europe.

By roughly 2000 B.C., various Celtic peoples, including the Belgae, were living throughout Belgium and in the southern Netherlands. Germanic groups inhabited the northern Netherlands, and contact between the Celtic and Germanic cultures was common. In fact, Germanic groups traveled into present-day Flanders in the first century B.C., intermarrying with the Celts. Southern Belgium (Wallonia), on the other hand, remained almost entirely Celtic.

Roman Rule

In the first century B.C., the Belgae, who were skilled warriors, fought the armies of the Roman Empire, which was expanding northward from southern Italy. From 58 to 51 B.C., the legions of the Roman general Julius Caesar conquered a wide area of northern Europe known as Gaul. The Romans eventually subdued the fierce Belgae and established the province of Belgica. This territory stretched from modern Belgium northward to the Rhine River, which runs through the present-day Netherlands and Germany.

The Romans set up army camps and built an extensive network of roads in Belgica, whose people paid taxes and provided troops. To feed their large army, the Romans established big farms to increase the province's grain harvest.

The Belgae easily adapted to Roman rule. Words from Latin, which the Romans spoke, entered the Celtic language of the Belgae. In the second century A.D., industry and trade flourished along the many waterways of Belgica. Several modern Belgian cities—such as Mons, Tournai, and Arlon—have Roman foundations.

By the end of the fourth century A.D., however, problems within the Roman government were weakening the empire's defenses. Germanic groups, particularly the Franks from central Europe, successfully attacked Roman holdings in Belgica. By

this time, the Romans had adopted the Christian faith as their official religion, and it began to spread to other parts of Europe.

Roman control of Belgica weakened further in the early A.D. 400s, when high tides in the North Sea flooded coastal lowlands along the Schelde estuaries. Areas farther inland became too marshy for continued farming, settlement, and defense, and Roman troops withdrew from their northern outposts.

The Frankish Empire

In 496 the Frankish leader Clovis defeated the Romans and ended their domination of Belgica. Some Roman influences, particularly the Christian religion and the Latin language, survived in parts of the Frankish kingdom. But the Roman style of government and the Roman legal code disappeared. By the early sixth century, Clovis had conquered additional lands to the south and east and had established the Merovingian dynasty (family of rulers). Clovis, who was a Christian king, sent missionaries to convert the non-Christian peoples throughout his realm. Christianity unified the different peoples and cultures in the far-flung Merovingian lands.

Childeric's son, Clovis, pushed the Romans out of Belgium in the late fifth century A.D. After setting out from Tournai, Clovis conquered more land and established the Merovingian dynasty (family of rulers).

In the southeastern province of Luxembourg, a statue commemorates Saint Willibrord, the missionary who helped to spread the Christian faith throughout Belgium in the late 600s.

By the eighth century, a new dynasty—called the Carolingians—had taken control from the Merovingians. Coming to power in 768, the Carolingian leader Charlemagne enlarged the kingdom and restored some Roman ways of governing. During his reign, the region near the Schelde River (now Flanders) became a major center of cloth production. Trading settlements were founded at Ghent, Brugge, Antwerp, Namur, and Liège. These centers handled goods from areas located farther up the Schelde and Meuse rivers. Charlemagne also strengthened his ties to the Roman Catholic pope, the leader of the Christian faith at that time.

Charlemagne's heirs divided the prosperous Frankish kingdom after his death in 814. During the next 100 years, Belgium passed into the hands of several Carolingian rulers. In 925 the East Frankish Kingdom (modern Germany) gained control of the region, which was then known as Lorraine.

During the ninth and tenth centuries, the people of Lorraine suffered attacks by Vikings from northern Europe. Sailing in swift longboats, the Vikings reached Flemish coastal towns, which the seafarers raided and then destroyed. Far removed from the center of German government, the people of Lorraine received little outside help in their struggle against the invaders. Local dukes, counts, and bishops, who felt only a weak loyalty for the German king, directed the building of forts and castles.

In time, the territories ruled by the nobles became strong, semi-independent states. By the eleventh century, they included the counties of Flanders, Hainaut-Holland, and Limburg, as well as the duchy (dukedom) of Brabant. Liège was a

A brilliant military leader, Charlemagne (Charles the Great) ruled a large part of western Europe in the eighth century. Through his efforts, the cultural, political, and economic life in his realm thrived. Charlemagne founded schools, built roads, established courts, and set up new industries.

At its height in the 1300s, Brugge was an international marketplace for the storage, import, and export of cloth, spices, wine, herring, and many other goods.

Photo by Daniel H. Condit

bishopric (a land governed by a bishop). Although the count of Flanders owed his loyalty to the king of France, the other provincial nobles pledged themselves to the German ruler.

The Growth of Cities

In the eleventh century, agriculture was the main activity in what is now Belgium, but trade was expanding rapidly along the country's rivers and coasts. Farmers built the first dikes and polders to reclaim soggy land from the sea. Permanent settlements developed near castles and monasteries. These new towns attracted laborers, merchants, and skilled craftspeople.

By the twelfth century, the merchants and craftspeople of the lowlands had organized guilds (trade associations) to advance their business interests. The guild members became active in local government, eventually influencing decisions made by the nobles about finances and about the defense of their towns.

Brugge and Antwerp were important trading hubs where local merchants bought and sold goods from England, Spain, Portugal, France, Italy, and the Baltic countries. These Belgian cities joined the Hanseatic League—a northern European political and trade organization. Merchants in Brugge exchanged Flemish cloth, French and German wines, and salt for grain, wood, tar, and furs from the east. A flourishing textile industry attracted weavers to the cities of Ghent and Ieper.

In return for the loyalty of wealthy citizens, nobles granted charters to the bigger towns. These documents listed the privileges and duties of the cities. Through their charters, the wealthy trading centers of Belgium became largely self-governing.

Burgundian Rule

In 1369 Margaret, the daughter and heiress of the powerful count of Flanders, married the duke of Burgundy, the French king's son. This union brought Flanders under the rule of Burgundy (now part of eastern France). Margaret's husband did not participate much in Flemish government, nor did his son and successor, the second duke.

20

The third duke of Burgundy, Philip the Good, took an active role in the affairs of the lowlands. During his long reign, from 1419 to 1467, Philip extended his realm southward and eastward to include Brabant, Hainaut-Holland, Namur, Luxembourg, and Antwerp. These provinces did not become a unified state but were loosely associated through their common loyalty to the duke.

To centralize his authority, Philip called representatives from the various provinces to Brussels in 1465. This assembly marked the beginning of the States-General, the future legislature of the Netherlands. Philip named his own council to make judicial and financial decisions in the lowland provinces. These changes took away powers that the provinces had once exercised.

Philip's son, Charles the Bold, inherited the duchy in 1467. Charles wanted to further unify and enlarge the Burgundian realm. To gain more territory, he waged almost continuous warfare against France. Charles heavily taxed the lowland provinces to pay for his military campaigns. The campaigns angered his neighbors in Germany, France, and Switzerland. They declared war on Charles, who was killed in battle in 1477.

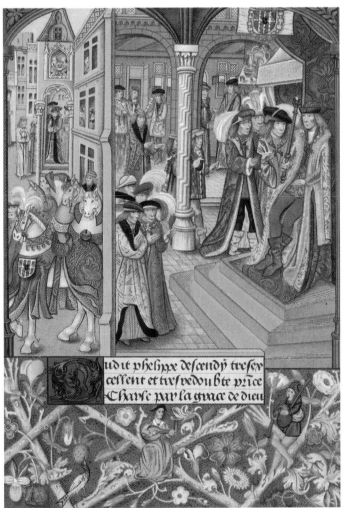

In the fifteenth century, the duchy (dukedom) of Burgundy included lands in Belgium. A hand-painted artwork shows Duke Charles *(right, sitting on throne)* consulting with his nobles and counselors. Although not a monarch, Charles was so powerful that he ran his domain without much interference from the king of France, to whom Charles owed his loyalty. When the citizens of Liège angered Charles in the 1460s, he ordered the city to be leveled by his forces, who left behind only the churches.

After Charles's death, the duchy of Burgundy became disorganized, and independence movements arose in the provinces. The expanding French kingdom threatened the stability of the lowlands. To escape a takeover by France, provincial leaders in Belgium and the Netherlands supported the claim of Mary, Charles's 20-year-old daughter. In return, she had to give back some of the provincial rights that Philip the Good had taken away. Mary also agreed to let the States-General meet at its own choosing rather than at the whim of the ruler.

The Early Habsburgs

Mary's control over the duchy of Burgundy increased—and the influence of the States-General declined—after she married Archduke Maximilian of Habsburg. The powerful Habsburgs, who were allied

Courtesy of The Cleveland Museum of Art, John L. Severance Fund

Through his marriage in 1477 to the heiress of the duchy of Burgundy, Maximilian of Habsburg gained control of Belgian lands. The Habsburgs maintained their authority in the region for more than 300 years.

with the Roman Catholic Church, ruled the Holy Roman Empire which covered much of central Europe at that time.

After Mary's sudden death in 1482, Maximilian governed her lands in the name of their young son, Philip, duke of Burgundy. The strongest Belgian cities—Brugge, Antwerp, and Ghent—resisted Burgundian rule in the late 1480s and early 1490s. To protect Philip's interests, Maximilian used force to crush the power of these cities.

Through the Habsburgs, the Burgundian rulers had a strong ally in the Roman Catholic Church. In the late fifteenth century, however, the church came under attack from religious leaders who believed it was becoming corrupt. These views fostered the Protestant Reformation, a movement to change the church's immoral practices. The Reformation eventually led to the establishment of independent Protestant churches in Germany and Switzerland. But Burgundy remained strongly Roman Catholic.

In 1496 Philip, who had grown up during these religious conflicts, married Joan, the daughter of the king of Spain, a Roman Catholic realm in southwestern Europe. By 1519 their son, Charles V, had inherited the Holy Roman Empire, which included Spain, the Burgundian duchy, and all the Habsburg lands in central Europe.

CHARLES V AND CALVINISM

When Charles V began his rule, Antwerp was one of the busiest trading centers in the western world. The port handled goods from Europe, from Spain's colonies in South America, and from Portugal's lands in West Africa. The Belgian textile industry had temporarily declined, but new foundries, tapestry weavers, and printing firms flourished.

Charles V enlarged his holdings by taking over most of the northern Netherlands and Flanders. Charles treated the lowland provinces—together called the Low Countries (now Belgium, the Netherlands, and

Tapestry weaving became a major economic activity in Belgium in the sixteenth century. Flemish weavers were particularly skilled at making these intricate wall hangings. The Flemish artisan Bernaert van Orley is thought to have designed this scene about the month of September, when traditionally grapes are harvested and are pressed to make wine.

Luxembourg)—as a semi-independent part of his vast domain. He established councils in each province to collect taxes and to direct day-to-day affairs.

During these years of economic growth and religious conflict, the people of Belgium had remained Roman Catholic. The ideas of the Protestant Reformation, how-ever, eventually reached the Low Countries through the writings and sermons of John Calvin. He preached a doctrine that urged hard work, simple tastes, and strict obedience to God's will.

In the 1540s, Calvinism spread to Antwerp, where Calvinists attempted to organize their own religious communities.

23

The Habsburg dynasty's heir Charles V inherited lands in Belgium in the early 1500s and later took over a vast realm that included territories in Spain, Germany, and central Europe. During Charles's 40-year reign, his armies successfully defended the empire from French and Turkish attacks and conquered new lands in Mexico and Peru.

Photo by Mansell Collection

Charles V and later Habsburg rulers saw Calvinism as a threat to their own power as well as to Roman Catholic authority.

Revolt Against Spain

Weary of his long reign and of religious disagreements, Charles gave up his throne in 1555. The Habsburg dynasty split into two branches. Charles's brother, who took over the Habsburg lands in central Europe, headed the Austrian branch. Charles's son, Philip II, led the Spanish branch of the family, becoming king of Spain and archduke of the Burgundian lowlands.

Philip had grown up in Spain with little understanding of Belgian ways. The new ruler stationed Spanish troops on Belgian territory and appointed Spaniards to administrative posts there. He heavily taxed the Belgian provinces and cities to pay for Spain's wars against France.

To strengthen the Catholic church, Philip created new Catholic districts in Belgium and gave land to Catholic bishops. He also authorized an inquisition (a trial held by church officials) against Calvinists. Protestant Belgians in Flanders, where the new faith had become strong, suffered imprisonment, exile, or execution because of their beliefs. To avoid arrest, many Belgian Calvinists fled the country.

Philip's policies in the lowlands grew so harsh that a group of Catholic and Protestant nobles put aside their religious differences and petitioned him for change. Led by William of Orange, a Protestant Dutch prince, the nobles asked King Philip to end the Inquisition, to grant religious freedom, and to assemble the States-General. One of Philip's advisers called these aristocratic petitioners "beggars," and, as the revolutionary movement grew, its backers defiantly adopted this name.

Although he was neither Belgian nor Catholic, the Dutch Protestant leader William of Orange won the trust of Belgian Catholics who wanted to end Habsburg rule.

Hurt by a declining textile industry and by soaring food prices, the common people supported the revolt by rioting and by destroying Roman Catholic property. Such actions rekindled the religious split and prevented a united stand against Spanish rule. Calvinists rallied around William of Orange, while Catholics supported rule by the Spanish Habsburgs.

In 1566 Philip sent the duke of Alva 10,000 troops to end the Calvinist revolution in the lowlands. To suppress the rebels, the duke set up a council that executed about 8,000 people. Through these harsh measures, the duke reestablished control in the Low Countries, but rebel forces continued to oppose him. In 1572 a group of Protestant refugees known as the Sea Beggars attacked Spanish ships and captured towns in the southern Netherlands. The success of the Sea Beggars prompted Dutch leaders to proclaim their country's independence from Spain.

In 1567 the duke of Alva *(center, on horseback),* **a noble employed by the Habsburg king Philip II, rode into Brussels with many soldiers. The duke's arrival marked the beginning of a period of religious and political repression in Belgium that was designed to crush opposition to Philip's power.**

Unity and Division

In response to rebel gains, Spanish troops sacked Antwerp in 1576. Angered by the destruction, Catholics and Protestants throughout the Netherlands and Belgium united to end Spanish rule. Before they could effectively oppose the Spaniards, however, the rebels had to resolve their religious differences. In 1576, therefore, the provincial representatives signed the Pacification (Peace) of Ghent, which recognized Catholicism as the official religion in most provinces in the Low Countries. Calvinism prevailed in Holland and Zeeland (now in the Netherlands).

In 1577 the provinces voted unanimously to reject the new Spanish governor—John of Austria—unless Philip agreed to withdraw all Spanish forces and to accept demands for religious freedom. To avoid further warfare, Philip consented to these conditions.

Unity among the provinces was short lived, however. Leaders in the southern provinces, which were mostly Catholic, remained suspicious of the Calvinists, who controlled the northern provinces. In 1579 several Catholic provinces in the south formed the Union of Arras and accepted the authority of the Spanish king. The split between northern and southern provinces deepened a few weeks later when the northern provinces united and announced their independence from Spain.

In the 1580s, the new Spanish governor, Alessandro Farnese, took advantage of the religious division in the Low Countries to conquer Ghent, Brussels, and Antwerp. In each case, Farnese allowed Protestants to leave the cities and move north. Spain was unsuccessful in its attempts to retake the northern provinces, which became the independent United Provinces of the Netherlands.

Industries in the United Provinces prospered, and port cities in the Netherlands soon outpaced Antwerp as centers of trade. Meanwhile, the economy of the southern, Spanish-held provinces wors-

Photo by Mansell Collection

Backed by King Philip, Alessandro Farnese (above) **took over Belgian cities during the rebellions of the late 1500s.**

ened as Spain demanded heavy taxes for its wars against the Dutch.

WARTIME DAMAGE

Just before his death in 1598, Philip II gave the Belgian provinces to his daughter as a marriage present. When she died without an heir in 1633, the region reverted to the Habsburg king of Spain, Philip IV. Philip brought the provinces into the final stages of the Thirty Years' War (1618–1648). In this conflict, France was attempting to stop the growth of the Habsburg Empire. The French and their allies, including the Dutch, finally defeated the Spanish forces in the 1640s.

These victories helped the Dutch to get favorable terms at the postwar peace conferences. For example, the treaty that ended the war gave some lands in Brabant and Flanders, including the Schelde estuaries, to the Netherlands. To secure their commercial domination of the region, the Dutch blockaded the port of Antwerp, an

In the 1600s, Belgium became the scene of conflicts between the Spanish Habsburgs and the French. This painting by the Flemish artist Adam Frans van der Meulen depicts a battle near a canal in Brugge in 1667.

The Spanish branch of the Habsburg dynasty died out in 1700. At the age of 23, Maria Theresa—the heiress to the Austrian branch—inherited Belgium. She ruled it with the intention of reviving its economy and improving social conditions.

action that further weakened Belgium's economy.

The ending of the Thirty Years' War did not stop hostilities on Belgian soil between France and Spain. During the second half of the seventeenth century, France annexed piece after piece of southern Belgium. In 1678 France captured the cities of Ieper and Ghent. In 1697 the Treaty of Ryswick finally ended French occupation of Belgium. Having served as a Franco-Spanish battleground for 50 years, much of southern Belgium was in ruins.

The 1700s

With the death in 1700 of Philip IV's heir, Charles II, the Spanish Habsburg dynasty ended. Disagreement over Charles's successor left Belgium's future uncertain. The rulers of France and Austria both claimed the Spanish throne, and the dispute resulted in the War of the Spanish Succession (1701–1714). After the war, the

27

Treaty of Utrecht awarded Belgium to the Austrian Habsburgs.

After inheriting the Austrian throne in 1740, Empress Maria Theresa adopted liberal policies in her lands. In Belgium, new social programs reformed the country's prison system and broadened opportunities for education. The Belgian economy revived as industries were modernized.

These policies mainly benefited the French-speaking population, which dominated government, business, and education. Even in the Flemish-speaking provinces of Flanders and Brabant, Catholic nobles and church officials used French, which was regarded as the language of well-educated people. This view lowered the status of people who spoke only Flemish.

Although Belgium's economy was still poor, Maria Theresa showed concern for

The lawyer Henri van der Noot led the unsuccessful movement to oust the Habsburgs from power in the late 1700s.

her subjects. Under her son Joseph II, however, Belgians suffered. His lack of sympathy for national and religious traditions disturbed the people.

Many conservative Belgian Catholics, led by Henri van der Noot, opposed Habsburg rule. They allied with a growing class of liberal merchants, lawyers, and doctors. The various groups rebelled against Austrian rule in 1789, but the revolt was short lived. Political and economic differences split the participants, making it easy for Joseph's successor to recapture the provinces in 1790.

French and Dutch Rule

In the late eighteenth century, French revolutionaries deposed their king and gained control of France. They also attempted to help other Europeans to overthrow their monarchs. In 1792 the French invaded Belgium and opened the

A snarling lion in an attacking pose adorns a provincial flag flying from a building in Dendermonde, East Flanders. The angry lion is an ancient Flemish symbol of defiance.

The French general Napoleon Bonaparte took over Belgium in 1795. By the early 1800s, he had conquered or had established control over most of Europe. His successes threatened many other European powers, who joined together to end Napoleon's reign.

Schelde River to Belgian trade. Directed by General Napoleon Bonaparte, French forces annexed the Belgian provinces on October 1, 1795.

The Napoleonic era brought some advantages to Belgium. The reopening of trade routes benefited Wallonia, especially Liège, where local deposits of iron ore

The Europeans allied against Napoleon finally stopped him on a battlefield in Belgium. A monument topped by a lion marks the spot at Waterloo, near Brussels, where in 1815 Napoleon was defeated. After the war, Belgium was combined with the Netherlands and Luxembourg.

Photo by INBEL-Brussels

supported the manufacture and export of weapons. Ghent's textile industry also expanded. The French reorganized the Belgian provinces, taking land away from the Catholic church and giving the holdings to farmers.

On the other hand, France heavily taxed the Belgians to finance French wars and restricted the use of the Flemish language. Napoleon's strong central government conflicted with the Belgians' drive for independence. The French anti-religious stance went against Belgium's Catholic traditions. The drafting of ordinary Belgians into the French army especially angered the common people.

By 1810 Napoleon had conquered most of mainland Europe. Hostility toward his ambitions united many European countries against him. An alliance of Austria, Britain, Prussia (now in Germany), Spain, and Russia pushed Napoleon's forces out of southern and central Europe. He met his final defeat in 1815 at Waterloo, a few miles south of Brussels.

The nations that overcame Napoleon decided Belgium's fate. Gathering at the Congress of Vienna in 1815, they drew new boundaries in Europe that they hoped would prevent France from rising to power again. Austria gave up its claims to the Belgian provinces in return for territory in Italy. The victors added Belgium and Luxembourg to the Netherlands.

The union of the Netherlands and the Belgian provinces failed, mainly because of religious and language differences. Belgians believed that the Protestant Dutch king, William I, was prejudiced against them. Despite an agreement that recognized their full equality, Belgians did not hold high offices and had fewer representatives in the States-General than the Dutch had.

When William attempted to remove schools from Catholic control, he angered both Flemish- and French-speaking Belgians. Flemings and Walloons set aside their age-old differences to oppose William. In 1828 the Dutch government attempted to suppress the Belgian press, which was criticizing William's policies. In response to this denial of freedom of speech, anti-Dutch organizations in Belgium formed the Union of Oppositions. The action of bringing together opposing groups helped Belgians to develop a sense of national identity and pride.

Belgian Independence

At first, Belgian leaders pressed for reforms in the Dutch government. But by 1830 a movement for complete independence from Dutch control was gaining momentum. In that year, economic problems caused urban workers to demonstrate for changes in the workplace. William sent troops to Brussels to put down these disturbances. The Dutch army withdrew after three days of heavy fighting, and within two weeks a temporary government had declared Belgium's independence.

Britain, a major European power at the time, supported Belgium's action in order to prevent another European war. To further strengthen Belgium's claims to self-rule, Britain arranged the Conference of London. At this meeting, other major European powers recognized Belgium's independence. In June 1831, a temporary Belgian parliament elected as king the

Photo by INBEL-Brussels

Belgians disliked the union with the Netherlands, and protests *(above)* erupted in Brussels in 1830. Belgian leaders *(left)* banded together later that year to proclaim the country's independence. They ran the government until the legislature elected a king.

Independent Picture Service

31

German prince Leopold of Saxe-Coburg, who was acceptable to both Britain and France.

Leopold I was satisfied to remain a constitutional monarch, a role that gave him very limited powers. Within these restrictions, however, he governed wisely and used his influence to further the economic interests of his adopted country. As a result, Belgium prospered as a self-ruling nation.

Belgian towns grew as the country's trade increased, and Antwerp again became a leading port. The mining of iron ore and coal in Wallonia fostered the growth of heavy industries, including the making of railway equipment and tram cars. By the mid-nineteenth century, manufactured goods had replaced agricultural products as the country's leading exports. These changes made Belgium the first nation on the European continent to become heavily industrialized.

LEOPOLD II

In 1865 Leopold II, the son of Leopold I, became king of Belgium. During his reign, the country developed a strong transportation network, stable financial institutions, and varied industries. These improvements brought vast riches to Belgium. Leopold II, however, wanted to increase his personal wealth by mining the resources of the African continent. He hired a British explorer named Henry Stanley to negotiate favorable treaties with African leaders in an area near the Congo (now Zaire) River. These agreements led to the establishment of the Congo Free State.

For 23 years, Leopold's personal control of the Congo brought him great wealth from its rubber and copper. In the early 1900s, however, reports that his officials in the Congo were torturing African workers caused global concern. An international commission pressured the Belgian parliament to end Leopold's personal authority in Africa. As a result, Belgium's government annexed the Congo in 1908 and took control of mining in the region. Thereafter, the Congo was run as a colony that belonged to the Belgian nation rather than to Leopold.

Despite Belgium's economic success, conflicts over language continued. French was used in government, business, and education. The Flemish people were unhappy with a system that did not give equal status to their language. In 1898, after public protests, Belgium officially became a bilingual (two-language) state, although governmental leaders continued to use French for many years.

The German prince Leopold of Saxe-Coburg became the first king of independent Belgium in 1831. He worked hard to promote Belgium's interests but remained faithful to the limits placed on his power by the Belgian constitution.

The World Wars

By the early twentieth century, Belgians were living in a stable but complex society

that was divided along political, religious, and language lines. People remained loyal to either their own religious group—the Catholics—or to a political faction, the Liberals. The Catholics and the Liberals each organized a separate, but parallel, grouping called a "pillar."

Each pillar was self-sufficient, having its own educational system, its own cultural institutions, its own trade unions, its own language, and even its own medical and social services. Within each pillar, separate political parties were formed to influence the government and to handle conflicts between the two pillars. Since organizations within each pillar dealt with the needs of its members, public discontent with the national government was largely avoided.

Most Belgians, regardless of their pillar, wanted economic stability and felt that peace in Europe was essential to achieve this aim. Diplomats in the previous century had set up international alliances to balance power among the major European nations. To avoid war, Belgium—like other small European countries—declared itself neutral, meaning it would not take sides in any military campaign. By 1914, however, the international agreements had failed to prevent conflict, and war broke out.

WORLD WAR I AND ITS AFTERMATH

World War I pitted the allied nations of Britain, France, Italy, and Russia against Germany and Austria. In August 1914, while pushing toward France, German forces invaded Belgium, violating its neutral status. The Belgians resisted, but only a strip of land in western Belgium remained in Belgian hands throughout the war.

In occupied territories, the war shattered local economies and ravaged the

Prolonged and bloody fighting during World War I (1914–1918) devastated Flanders. This road, which ran through the village of Poelkapelle in West Flanders, had become little more than a dirt track by 1918.

The rapid defeat of Belgium during World War II (1939–1945) again destroyed the countryside and left many women and children homeless.

countryside. Ieper alone was the scene of three major battles. Hundreds of thousands of soldiers lost their lives during prolonged campaigns in southern Belgium and northern France. Thousands of Belgians fought with the Allies until Germany's defeat in 1918.

After the conflict, Belgium helped to found the League of Nations, an international assembly whose goal was the prevention of future wars. The league awarded Belgium the German colonies of Ruanda and Urundi in Africa (present-day Rwanda and Burundi). The Treaty of Versailles, which formally ended World War I, gave Belgium the German areas of Eupen, Malmédy, and St. Vith (now in eastern Liège province).

A worldwide economic depression in the 1930s undermined Belgium's efforts to rebuild its ruined economy. Throughout most of Europe, unemployment was high, and many people struggled to survive. Harsh political regimes that promised law, order, and economic stability arose. Nazism, the most powerful of these movements, flourished in Germany under the direction of Adolf Hitler. In Belgium, however, the monarchy remained stable under Leopold III, who inherited the crown in 1934.

WORLD WAR II

Germany's military buildup in the 1930s threatened to end peace in Europe. In 1936, to avoid attack, Belgium again proclaimed its neutrality. Britain, France, and Germany recognized Belgium's neutral stance. Germany's takeover of nearby countries, however, made conflict likely, and by 1939 World War II had begun. On May 10, 1940—despite its pledge to honor Belgium's neutrality—Germany again invaded Belgium while pushing toward France.

After 18 days of bitter fighting, Leopold III arranged for the Belgian army to surrender. The king remained in command of the nation's forces, but some Belgians felt he had given up too soon. After Nazi troops occupied the country, Germany stripped Belgium of money, goods, and workers. Belgians organized an underground resistance movement, and some units of the Belgian armed forces escaped to Britain, where they joined the alliance against Germany.

The German occupation lasted until the summer of 1944, when a massive allied invasion of northern France led to the liberation of Belgium. In December 1944, the retreating Germans launched their final offensive in the Ardennes during the Battle of the Bulge. Germany surrendered in May 1945.

Because Leopold III had surrendered to Germany early in the war, Belgium was spared much of the destruction that took place in some other parts of Europe. Nevertheless, many Belgians felt the king had been too helpful to Hitler. The issue sharpened the division between the Flemings —who generally supported the monarch— and the Walloons, who demanded that he give up his throne. Leopold lived outside Belgium during the troubled postwar years and resigned his office in 1951. His son Baudouin I succeeded him.

Postwar Recovery

Despite internal conflicts between Flemings and Walloons, Belgium generally prospered in the postwar period. With foreign aid, the country updated its manufacturing sector. Most improvements occurred in Flanders, where international investors updated and expanded industries. In Wallonia, however, there was little improvement in industrial activity.

Women received the right to vote in 1948, a privilege that men had had since 1919. The Belgian government expanded the nation's social-welfare programs, which protected citizens from economic hardship through pensions, health insurance, and unemployment benefits.

King Baudouin and Belgium's other political leaders organized efforts to increase

King of Belgium since 1951, Baudouin I has used his influence to foster unity within Belgium as well as among the nations of Europe.

By 1958 Belgium had begun to recover economically and hosted the World's Fair in Brussels. *The Atomium*, a sculpture representing an atom of iron, still stands as a reminder of the event.

The administrative headquarters of the North Atlantic Treaty Organization (NATO) is in Brussels. This defensive alliance formed after World War II to confront uncertain political conditions in Europe. NATO's member-countries each send permanent delegations to the NATO council, which is always in session in Brussels.

Courtesy of NATO

international cooperation. Belgium became a founding member of the United Nations (UN), an international agency that works toward world peace. Belgium also made commercial agreements with the Netherlands and Luxembourg. Together called the Benelux union, these three small countries in the lowlands gained economic strength. They also joined the North Atlantic Treaty Organization (NATO)—a defensive military alliance to which most other western European countries also belong. NATO has its administrative headquarters in Brussels, and the alliance's military headquarters is near the Belgian city of Mons.

The success of the Benelux union inspired greater economic cooperation among other European countries. The Common Market, later called the European Community (EC), began in 1957, and made Brussels its administrative headquarters. The EC coordinates trade policies for all member-nations and provides investment funds to foster economic growth among EC partners.

In the 1960s, a UN resolution encouraged European countries to grant self-rule to their colonies. After unrest erupted in

the Belgian Congo (now called Zaire), Belgium quickly agreed to the territory's independence in 1960 and to self-rule for Rwanda and Burundi in 1962.

After giving up its colonies, Belgium maintained a prosperous economy, but deep divisions still existed in Belgian society. By 1970 economic differences— particularly between the Flemish- and French-speaking people of Belgium—had grown sharper. Flemish-speaking Flanders flourished in the 1970s as multinational companies built modern manufacturing plants and new communications networks. In contrast, French-speaking Wallonia declined because of its outdated heavy industries and exhausted coal mines. This region did not receive much foreign aid or investment in the postwar era.

The Walloons, who felt that the national government was ignoring their needs, argued for the division of the nation into two independent regions. The Flemings, who did not want to be financially responsible for Wallonia, also supported the idea of division.

In response to this dilemma, Belgians voted several times in the 1970s and 1980s to alter their constitution. The constitu-

The Town Hall in Mons, the capital of the Wallonian province of Hainaut, dates from the 1400s. The city is also the Supreme Headquarters of Allied Powers in Europe (SHAPE), NATO's military arm.

tional changes created regional assemblies, appointed governing boards, and divided investment funds among the main language regions. Amendments in 1989 made Belgium a three-part federal state in which Flanders, Wallonia, and Brussels gained powers that formerly belonged to the national government.

Recent Events

The division between Flemings and Walloons has caused the development of small, regional political parties. National governments are formed by coalitions (temporary combinations) of the parties that collectively hold a majority in the Belgian parliament. The Flemish Christian People's party—the largest political organization in Flanders—is allied with a smaller, like-minded party in Wallonia. Together the two parties make up a Catholic voting bloc.

The Christian People's party has provided several recent prime ministers, including Leo Tindemans and Wilfried Martens. Martens has been reelected several times since he first took office in 1979. The Socialists, who are strong in

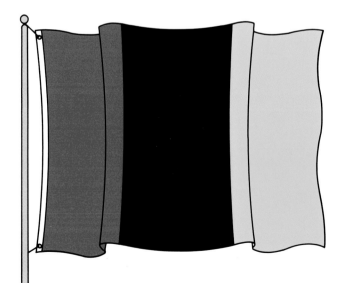

The design of the Belgian national flag is based on the three-part French flag. The colors on the Belgian standard, however, are taken from the banner of the ancient dukes of Brabant who lived near Brussels. Almost all provincial flags in Belgium —whether in Flanders or in Wallonia —also use red, black, and yellow.

Photo by INBEL-Brussels

Wilfried Martens, head of the Christian People's party, began his first term as Belgium's prime minister in 1979.

Wallonia, have Flemish- and French-speaking political wings, as do the Liberals, whose focus of support is in Brussels.

Martens successfully steered Belgium through the difficult economic times of the 1980s, when the government was deeply in debt. In that decade, one-seventh of Belgium's annual income was used to pay interest on its debt, which resulted partly from generous spending on public-welfare programs. In addition, unemployment and the price of goods were on the rise.

In the late 1980s, the government granted Martens emergency powers to improve the country's financial standing. The prime minister adopted severe economic measures. He slashed public spending and social-welfare benefits to reduce the growth of the national debt. Workers had to take pay cuts, which caused demonstrations and strikes (work stoppages).

Martens lowered taxes on industries so they could boost their output, could become more competitive on the world market, and could create new jobs.

To achieve his goals, Martens had to weather the short-term collapse of his government and the building of new political coalitions. By the early 1990s, the strong measures seemed to be working, and Belgium's economic outlook was more hopeful than it had been for many years.

Another important event during Martens's terms of office has been the EC's plans to form a unified trading bloc by the mid-1990s. As the headquarters of the EC's policy-making wing, Brussels and Belgium are at the center of these broad changes in the European marketplace.

Government

Belgium is a parliamentary democracy under a constitutional monarch. In theory, executive power rests with the monarch and the Belgian cabinet, called the Council of Ministers. In practice, the monarch has very limited power, and all major decisions are made by the ministers. The prime minister is the head of the council, which remains in power as long as it has the confidence of the Belgian parliament. The monarch does have a guiding role in the formation of coalitions and, with the prime minister's approval, names the members of the Council of Ministers.

Parliament, which consists of a house of representatives and a senate, exercises legislative authority. Parliamentary elections take place at least once every four years. The people directly elect the 212 members of the House of Representatives, the dominant body in the legislature. Of the 183 senators, 106 are directly elected, 51 are chosen by provincial councils, and 26 are appointed by fellow senators. The heir to the Belgian throne also is a member of the Senate.

The highest court in the Belgian judicial system is the Court of Cassation, whose

The Belgian senate meets in an elegant semicircular chamber in Brussels. Not all of the senate's members are elected, and King Baudouin's heir—his nephew Philippe—also can attend sessions.

Independent Picture Service

chief justice is chosen by the cabinet. Assize (inquest) courts, which operate at the provincial level, handle major civil and criminal cases and are the only Belgian tribunals with juries. Courts of appeal hear cases that come from lower courts or that involve offenses by public officials. District tribunals headed by justices of the peace hear minor civil and criminal cases.

The three regions of Belgium—Flanders, Wallonia, and Brussels— have strong governments elected by the people of each region. Regional leaders have authority over economic, social, and administrative matters, but they also cooperate with officials in Belgium's nine provincial governments. Each province has its own council and its own governor, who is chosen by the Council of Ministers.

A war memorial in Brussels points to the huge Palace of Justice, where Belgium's highest courts meet.

Independent Picture Service

Photo © James Alan Brown/Visuals Unlimited

Belgians enjoy festivals throughout the year. At Stavelot, a town in Liège province, a masked woman leads a group of colorfully clothed Walloons in a pre-Easter celebration.

3) The People

With nearly 10 million people, Belgium is one of the most densely populated nations in Europe. Almost all Belgians live in towns, cities, and suburbs, but population densities in the nation vary greatly. Brussels and Antwerp record nearly 3,000 people per square mile, while some rural parts of the Ardennes have less than 130 inhabitants per square mile.

Birthrates also differ between the country's two main regions. Flanders has a high rate of population growth and very little emigration. Wallonia, on the other hand, has a negative birthrate, and the population of native-born Walloons is de-

creasing. Foreigners coming into the area, however, have kept Wallonia's overall numbers stable.

Ethnic Identity and Social Structure

Flanders and Wallonia are the centers of Belgium's ethnic and language groups. The Flemings live in the western and northern provinces of West Flanders, East Flanders, Antwerp, and Limburg, and in the northern part of Brabant. The southern part of Brabant has ties to Wallonia, whose other provinces are Hainaut, Namur, Liège, and Luxembourg.

40

The ethnic background of Flemings and Walloons is almost identical. Both groups are descended from Celts (the Belgae) and Germanic peoples (mainly the Franks). Germanic and Celtic cultures intermingled in Flanders, where the people adopted Flemish, a dialect of Germanic origin. In Wallonia, the ethnic identity was more strictly Celtic. During the Roman era, the Celts gradually adopted Latin—the Roman language—which evolved, in this area of Europe, into French.

About 56 percent of Belgium's citizens speak only Flemish, 32 percent speak only French, and 11 percent use both languages. Less than 1 percent of Belgians are German-speakers who live in the eastern part of Liège province, which borders Germany.

Within Belgium's two major regions, people have organized their societies into separate, self-sufficient pillars that guide

In Brussels, a chef shows off his impressive array of seafood dishes.

These young Flemings are part of the Procession of the Cats, which is held every other May in Ieper.

nearly all areas of life. Each pillar has its own political parties, unions, newspapers, schools, and social organizations. Through the pillar system, members find jobs, arrange medical care, and conduct business.

People who share similar religious and political beliefs usually belong to the same pillar. As a result, for a Belgian to shift loyalty from one pillar to another would mean more than just switching to a different political party. A wide range of social contacts would also be changed.

Three pillars—Catholic, Liberal, and Socialist—exist in Belgium. The Catholic pillar crosses all social lines, combining upper, middle, and working classes. It has a French-speaking and a Flemish-speaking political party to represent members from both language groups. The Liberal pillar is made up mainly of middle-class professionals, and the Socialist pillar is dominated by workers. Both of these pillars also have Flemish and French wings in their political parties.

Religion

Although almost all Belgians are baptized as Roman Catholics, the Belgian constitution recognizes several other faiths, including Islam, Judaism, and Protestantism. Membership in non-Catholic sects, however, is small.

The Roman Catholic Church strongly influences the lives and politics of some Belgians. Most communities celebrate Catholic saints' days and hold a variety of Roman Catholic ceremonies in public. Catholic clergy usually officiate at marriages, baptisms, and funerals.

Despite their Catholic heritage, not all modern Belgians practice their faith. In

Photo by UPI/Bettmann Newsphotos

Charges of inequality between French-speakers and Flemish-speakers have sparked demonstrations in several Belgian cities. Here, Flemings give a victory salute after entering a section of Brussels where Flemish is not widely used.

Most Belgians, whether Flemings or Walloons, are members of the Roman Catholic Church. Wayside Catholic shrines, such as this example in the Ardennes, are common along secondary roads.

general, Walloons are not as strict about attending religious services as Flemings are. In recent years, the population has sometimes disagreed with positions taken by the church on political and social issues. The Liberals and the Socialists, for example, oppose the church's anti-abortion stance. The parties of the Catholic bloc, on the other hand, usually support mainstream Catholic positions.

Muslims, who follow the religion of Islam, are the largest non-Christian group in Belgium. Most of Belgium's 200,000 Muslims emigrated from Turkey and North Africa to find jobs. Many Belgian Jews either left the country or were killed during World War II. The remainder of this religious community, which is centered in Brussels and Antwerp, numbers about 35,000.

Education

Language differences also affect Belgium's educational system. Instruction is in either Flemish or French, depending on the region. Virtually all Belgians can read and write in at least one of the national languages.

Belgian children must attend school until the age of 16. The government funds both public and private schools, and tuition is free. Fifty-seven percent of young Belgians attend private schools, most of which are run by religious groups. Secondary schools offer courses in general, technical, artistic, and vocational studies.

Belgium has many schools for advanced technical and vocational training as well as six universities. The oldest institution of higher education is the Catholic University of Louvain, which was founded in 1425. Its world-famous library is rich in materials from the Middle Ages (the sixth to the sixteenth centuries). Once bilingual, the Catholic University of Louvain was divided into independent Flemish- and French-speaking parts in 1970.

Founded in 1834, the Free University of Brussels has no religious ties but does have

43

Belgian students wrestle in the playing field near their school. About half of the nation's children go to private schools that are run by the Catholic church. Instruction is either in French or in Flemish, depending on the school's location.

independent Flemish and French wings. Other Belgian universities opened in the nineteenth and twentieth centuries. Professors at the state-run university at Ghent, established in 1917, teach in Flemish. The schools at Liège and Mons offer their courses in French.

Health and Welfare

All Belgians—no matter what their language group—benefit from their country's social-security system. The national health insurance system, which is funded by employers and employees, covers medical and dental expenses. When they retire, Belgian workers receive pensions equal to about 60 percent of their average yearly earnings. Employees get part of their regular salary when they are sick, and other programs provide incomes for people with disabilities and injuries and for the unemployed.

Although the standard of living in Belgium is fairly high, inequalities exist. Once rich in coal and iron-ore deposits, Wallonia has declined as its major industries have become costly to maintain. Meanwhile, commerce and high-technology manufacturing have developed in Flanders. This shift has given Flemings a higher standard of living than Walloons. Many young Walloons have gone to other regions—especially to Brussels—to find jobs.

Partly because of the nation's strong health-care system, Belgians have good health statistics overall. The country's citizens have an average life expectancy of 74 years, which is slightly lower than the figures in other countries of western Europe. The infant mortality rate of 9 deaths in every 1,000 live births is a bit higher than in neighboring countries. Compared to many other parts of the world, however, these rates show that Belgians live long and healthy lives.

44

Visual Arts

Belgium's massive cathedrals, which were begun in the 1200s, stimulated the development of the nation's visual arts. In the fourteenth century, an artistic movement called Flemish primitivism flourished in the prosperous cities of Flanders. While experimenting with light and color, Flemish primitive painters also turned their attention away from traditional religious themes toward a broader range of human activity.

Among the movement's greatest artists was Jan van Eyck. His canvases give a detailed view of everyday life in the 1300s and 1400s. Van Eyck used rich colors, precise drawings, and natural lighting to portray his subjects. These techniques influenced many later European artists.

Roger van der Weyden, a contemporary of Jan van Eyck, produced works that reveal strong emotions. Van der Weyden's graceful arrangement of figures and his attention to detail give his portraits and

Photo by Drs. A. A. M. van der Heyden, Naarden, the Netherlands

The many panels of Jan van Eyck's masterpiece *Adoration of the Lamb* hang in Ghent's fifteenth-century cathedral. A detail of the work shows a group of female musicians.

Courtesy of Minneapolis Public Library and Information Center

In his portrait of an unknown lady, Roger van der Weyden leaves us an exact record of how women dressed in the 1400s.

Courtesy of Minneapolis Public Library and Information Center

This small part of Pieter Brueghel's *The Wedding Dance* shows the artist's interest in the world of Belgium's common people in the 1500s.

In about 1639, a year before he died, Peter Paul Rubens painted this self-portrait. It shows him as a confident man in his early sixties. Rubens not only created an astounding number of artworks but also designed books, buildings, and sculptures. In addition, he was a respected diplomat who undertook sensitive negotiations between England and Spain for the Spanish Habsburgs. Married twice and the father of eight children, Rubens enjoyed a long and prosperous career. In his later life, he stayed close to his estate near Brussels, producing canvases that reflected his fondness for the landscape of his native Flanders.

religious scenes unusual depth. His work influenced the German-born artist Hans Memling, who lived in Brugge after 1466. Memling's portraits express warmth and strength. In the same period, Hugo van der Goes created several large altarpieces that vividly portray religious figures. Belgium's greatest sixteenth-century painter was Pieter Brueghel, who was inspired by the robust world of peasants and by the changing seasons of the year.

Peter Paul Rubens (1577–1640) used a brilliant range of colors to create powerful scenes of everyday life. He organized a busy workshop of apprentices, who roughed out paintings to which Rubens later added his own distinctive touches. More than 2,000 portraits, peasant scenes, and religious works have been attributed to Rubens and his studio.

Among Rubens's assistants was Antwerp-born Anthony Van Dyck, who became a famous portrait painter in the 1600s. Van Dyck, who was hired by kings and nobles throughout Europe, painted people in elegant, dignified poses.

Two modern Belgian artists, James Ensor (1860–1949) and René Magritte

Courtesy of Musée National du Louvre

Anthony Van Dyck, an assistant of Rubens, painted this hunting portrait of King Charles I of England. Silhouetted against the sky, the king looks relaxed and elegant. King Charles later awarded Van Dyck a knighthood.

Photo by INBEL-Brussels

At a public gathering shortly before his death in 1967, René Magritte signed autographs. His surrealist works of art force viewers to look at ordinary objects in a completely new way.

47

(1898–1967), are noted for their impact on surrealism. Surrealist painters expressed images as they might appear in dreams. Ensor helped to start the surrealist movement through his paintings and etchings of scary and gruesome nightmares. Magritte's placement of realistic objects within dreamlike fantasies distinguished him from other surrealists of his time.

Literature and Music

Belgium has a long literary tradition in both the French and Flemish languages. In general, Walloons have written in French, and Flemings have made contributions in both French and Flemish. Historically, French has been the dominant language in Belgian literature, partly because most of the country's educated people—nobles, clergy, and wealthy merchants—used it.

BELGIAN LITERATURE IN FRENCH

In the thirteenth and fourteenth centuries, French-speaking writers in Liège produced mystery plays, which were based on stories from the Bible. Long ballads and folk songs were also popular works. During the same period, Flemings composed tales in French to entertain the counts of Flanders.

A statue at Damme, the ancient port of Brugge, honors Tijl Ulenspiegel, a Flemish fictional character known for his stamina and bravery. Stories about Ulenspiegel first appeared in the late 1400s. In the 1800s, a new twist on his adventures made the Flemish hero a member of the Sea Beggars, who fought to free Belgium from Spanish rule in the 1500s.

Photo by Drs. A. A. M. van der Heyden, Naarden, the Netherlands

48

Born in Ghent, the writer Maurice Maeterlinck authored a wide variety of works, ranging from the tragic drama *Pelléas and Mélisande* to a scientific study of the life of bees.

Belgium's output of works in French declined for several centuries during social and military upheavals. In the late 1800s, however, money from wealthy Belgian citizens funded a revival of literary activity that benefited authors such as Octave Pirmez and Maurice Maeterlinck. Pirmez wrote mystical prose, and Maeterlinck was a poet, essayist, and playwright. Maeterlinck won the Nobel Prize for literature in 1911 for his plays, the most famous of which is *The Blue Bird*.

In the twentieth century, Emile Verhaeren conveyed views about Belgian society in his French-language poetry. The Belgian poet Charles Plisnier was the first foreigner to win the Goncourt Prize, one of France's highest literary awards. The Liège-born author Georges Simenon used penetrating psychological insights in his popular mysteries, which feature Police Inspector Maigret. Françoise Mallet-Joris raises feminist issues in her novels, which include *Le rempart des Béguines*.

Writing in French, the Belgian novelist Georges Simenon probed the complex psychology of his characters.

Born in Antwerp but now living in Paris, the Belgian poet and author Françoise Mallet-Joris has produced many novels, including *La chambre rouge* (The Red Bedroom) and *Lettre à moi-même* (Letter to Myself).

BELGIAN LITERATURE IN FLEMISH

Flemish literature became popular among the educated and wealthy classes as early as the fourteenth century, when the mystical and religious writings of Jan van Ruysbroeck appeared. Petrus Dorlandus wrote the Flemish folktale *Elckerlyc* in the late 1400s. For several hundred years, political upheavals lessened Flemish literary contributions.

In the 1800s, the historical novels of Hendrik Conscience, including *The Lion of Flanders,* furthered recognition of Flemish literature. The world wars in the twentieth century inspired the rural novels of Felix Timmermans and the psychological works of Maurice Roelants and Johan Daisne.

BELGIAN MUSIC

Belgian influences on western European music date to at least the 1300s, when Liège

Photo by INBEL-Brussels

In the 1800s, the writings of Hendrik Conscience revived the interest of Flemings in their own history, language, and literature.

Photo by Bettmann Archive

The religious music of the Flemish composer Orlando di Lasso was popular throughout the 1500s. He traveled widely in Europe, working for nobles in Germany and Italy.

became famous for its choirs that sang in four- and five-part harmony. The Burgundian court of the 1400s and 1500s sponsored musical composition, including the nonreligious songs of Guillaume Dufay and the religious music of Orlando di Lasso and Philippe de Monte. Adriaan Willaert, who worked mostly in Italy in the 1500s, was one of the first European composers of purely instrumental music.

Born in the nineteenth century in Liège were the violinist Eugène-Auguste Ysaÿe and the composer César Auguste Franck. Ysaÿe not only played the violin but also conducted orchestras and composed operas. Franck achieved enduring fame for his organ and symphonic music, particularly the Symphony in D Minor. Paul Gilson, whose best-known work is *La Mer* (The Sea), dominated Belgian music in the early twentieth century. Born in Brussels in 1929, Jacques Brel became a popular singer and songwriter in the 1950s and 1960s. His lyrics often criticized modern morals, and he enjoyed a wide following in both Europe and North America.

Food

The preparation and enjoyment of food is an important part of daily life in Belgium. The Belgian diet typically contains a great variety of seafood—including shrimp, eels, and various smoked or fresh fish. Steamed mussels, flavored with seaweed and leeks, are a Belgian staple, as are *frites* (french fries). Belgian endive, a white-leafed lettuce, and asparagus grown in the sandy soil of Kempenland are also standard items in Belgian cooking. Beef, which is the most popular red meat in the country, is used in a tasty stew cooked in Flemish beer.

The country's butcher shops prepare many types of sausages and cured meats. During hunting season, cooks serve game

A worker soaks and cleans heads of endive, a white-leafed vegetable that is very popular throughout Belgium.

Courtesy of Belgian National Tourist Office, New York

Courtesy of Belgian National Tourist Office, New York

Two young Belgians clutch containers of *frites* (french fries), which are sold from food stalls all over the country.

51

Independent Picture Service

In Namur province, where the limestone plateau of the Ardennes begins, climbers have many opportunities to tackle the cliffs.

—including goose, venison (deer meat), hare, and boar—that come from the forests of the Ardennes. With their meal, adults often choose one of Belgium's 300 domestic varieties of beer. Wines imported from France and Luxembourg are also popular. Belgians argue that their chocolate is the best in the world.

Sports and Festivals

The people of Belgium are enthusiastic athletes and sports spectators. The country's North Sea coast is lined with resort towns that draw many foreign visitors as well as Belgians. The hills and valleys of the Ardennes offer opportunities for hiking, hunting, fishing, and cave exploration.

Soccer and bicycle racing are the most popular spectator sports in Belgium. Belgians take a keen interest in European bicycle races, especially the Tour de France. Young Belgians play *pelote*, a fast-

Photo by INBEL-Brussels

The finals of the Belgian *pelote* championships are held in Brussels. The fast-paced game resembles handball and is played throughout the nation.

paced game of skill and strength that resembles handball. Fitness activities, such as weight lifting, aerobics, jogging, swimming, and cycling, are also very popular in modern Belgium.

Folk festivals take place throughout the country. These celebrations, which often last several days or weeks, can be quite elaborate. The four-week pre-Easter carnivals in Wallonia, for example, feature colorfully dressed figures who parade and dance. A special part of spring festivities in Ath, a town in Hainaut province, is the Giants' Fair, when huge figures walk on stilts through the streets.

Flemings salute historical and religious events throughout the year. Citizens of Pieter Brueghel's hometown of Wingene celebrate his genius by reenacting scenes from his paintings. Harvest festivals occur in the autumn months, leading up to a variety of Christmas observances in December and January.

During a festival in the capital, a folk group from Namur performs on stilts.

Held in Brussels's Grand Place in July, the Ommegang pageant features large historic figures that reenact past events.

With the help of an overhead crane, Belgian workers guide large plates of glass onto a stationary rack.

4) The Economy

Belgium entered the 1980s with serious economic problems. Long dependent on international trade, the country faced a declining demand for its traditional products. The national debt had grown partly because of years of high government spending. Prices for consumer goods increased rapidly, and unemployment rose.

During the decade, the government took measures to restore the country's economic health. Tax cuts for businesses helped industries to boost their output and to become more competitive internationally. Many workers and managers had to accept pay decreases. Reductions in public spending and in social-welfare benefits enabled the government to lessen the amount of money it borrowed from international banks.

As a result of these measures, the Belgian economy had shown significant improvement by the early 1990s. Industries were more competitive, and the unemployment rate had fallen from 14 percent in

1983 to about 9 percent in 1991. In addition, Belgians seemed prepared to accept a temporary lowering of their standard of living to achieve long-term economic stability.

Industry

After World War II, light manufacturing and chemical industries developed rapidly in Flanders, and high-technology industries followed in the 1970s and 1980s. On the other hand, Wallonia, which was economically strong in the 1800s, struggled to survive in the same decades. Its mines are now nearly depleted, and its outdated heavy industries need massive investments to modernize.

Belgian factories use imported iron and steel to make many types of metal goods, including surgical instruments, sheet metal, railway gear, and oil-drilling equipment. Textiles are another major manufactured product in Belgium. Flemish flax plants provide the raw material for linen cloth, but wool, cotton, and other fibers are purchased abroad to make finished clothing. Carpets made from synthetic materials are a leading Belgian export.

Belgium's large glassmaking businesses contribute to the prosperity of Liège, Mons, and Charleroi. The chemical industry, which has been important to the national economy for more than a century, ranks as one of modern Belgium's most vital manufacturing sectors. It produces fertilizers, plastics, pharmaceuticals, cleaners, and photographic materials. Antwerp remains a leading center for the production of industrial diamonds, drawing much of its supply of uncut gems from Africa.

A long tradition of fine crafting survives in Belgium alongside advanced technology. Buyers prize handmade Belgian lace, both for the variety of its patterns and for the delicacy of its needlework. Other Belgian craftspeople produce attractive leather goods, including gloves and handbags. Skilled ironworkers create wrought-iron

Courtesy of Belgian National Tourist Office, New York

A technician at a crystal factory uses industrial machinery to cut facets into a goblet.

Courtesy of Belgian National Tourist Office, New York

An artisan in Brugge makes a piece of fine bobbin lace by carefully twisting and tying off threads that are wound around small bobbins.

furniture and scrolled ornamentation for buildings. Many gun experts rank the custom-made firearms from Liège among the best in the world. Bookbinding is also a traditional Belgian craft.

Trade

Belgium's location between large, wealthy nations and the sea has made trade important to the economy. More than half of the country's industrial output is sold abroad. Despite its small size, Belgium ranks high among exporting and importing nations.

Belgium's leading exports include machinery, gems, refined petroleum products, iron and steel goods, chemicals, carpets, copper, vehicle parts, and pharmaceuticals. The nation must import many of the raw materials needed by its industries. Belgium's chief imports are motor vehicles, chemicals, and foodstuffs. The country's main trading partners are Germany, France, and the Netherlands.

Belgium is one of the founders of the European Community (EC), an economic organization that sets trade policies for its member-nations. The country actively participates in the effort to create a single

1987 Per Capita GNP in U.S. Dollars

Under $3,000
$3,000–$9,000
$9,000–$12,000
$12,000–$15,000
$15,000–$22,000

Artwork by Laura Westlund

This map compares the average productivity per person—calculated by gross national product (GNP) per capita—for 26 European nations. The GNP is the value of all goods and services produced by a nation in a year. To arrive at the GNP per capita, each nation's total GNP is divided by its population. The resulting dollar amounts are one measure of the standard of living in each country. In 1987, as the Belgian economy was gradually improving, the per-capita income was $11,360. Belgium's trade with partners in the European Community is already causing this figure to rise. (Data taken from *Europa World Yearbook, 1989*.)

Pointed stacks of flax crowd the fields of a farm in West Flanders. The plants provide the raw material for linen weaving.

Nearly 30,000 glass greenhouses in Brabant are devoted to the growing of grapes. The fruit, which requires hot weather, would not survive outdoors in Belgium.

European market. Trade barriers have fallen between members, permitting the free flow of merchandise and labor in the EC. In addition, the EC sets quotas for the production of some items, such as steel and food.

Agriculture, Forestry, and Fishing

Only about 3 percent of Belgians work in the agricultural sector. Belgian farms meet 80 percent of the country's food needs, and some surplus goods are exported. In general, Belgian farms are small, and their owners' incomes have not grown in recent years. Subsidies (payments to make up for low prices) from the EC have helped Belgian farmers to survive.

The country's leading farm products are flax, vegetables, flowering plants, livestock, cereals, sugar beets, and potatoes. The lowlands of northern Belgium have sandy soil, which is suited to the cultivation of potatoes, asparagus, and grains. Flax thrives in West Flanders. In the polders—areas that were once marshes— Flemish farmers grow grasses to feed their livestock.

Fields of begonias are part of central Belgium's output of horticultural crops. These flowering herbs are sold both within the country and abroad.

The heavily forested Ardennes supplies Belgium's paper and construction industries with needed raw materials.

58

A cart *(left)* **holds fish and shellfish caught in the North Sea, where a fisherman** *(right)* **works close to shore with the help of his horse.**

Farms in central Belgium specialize in dairy products, orchard crops, and wheat. Large greenhouses that cultivate fruits and flowers dot the landscape. From this middle zone also come substantial harvests of oats, barley, and sugar beets. The Ardennes is especially suited to raising cattle. Apart from cattle and horses, the principal farm animals raised in Belgium are pigs, chickens, and rabbits.

Forestry is a profitable activity in parts of southeastern Belgium, especially in the province of Luxembourg. Nearly half of the province is forested, and much of the land is under the management of a government agency. Pine, spruce, and larch are harvested to supply Belgium's building and paper industries.

Although it lies along the North Sea, Belgium does not have a large fishing industry. The country's main fishing ports are at Oostende and Zeebrugge. The fishing fleets mainly supply the local demand

for seafood, which is used in many regional and national dishes. Herring and several varieties of flatfish are the principal catches. Most other popular species must be imported.

Energy and Mining

Coal, which supplied 90 percent of Belgium's energy in 1960, now accounts for only 10 percent. Declining coal stocks and increased use of oil help to explain this shift. Imported oil meets two-thirds of the nation's energy needs. Almost all of the country's petroleum comes from the Middle East, making Belgium vulnerable to changes in world oil prices and supplies. The nation also buys large amounts of natural gas from Norway, Algeria, the Netherlands, and the Soviet Union. In the 1980s, Belgium expanded its use of nuclear power to generate about 60 percent of its electricity.

59

Coal mining once thrived in several parts of Belgium. The industry has declined as stocks have dropped, but some mining still takes place in Flanders.

With the country's uncertain access to oil, Belgium may return to the heavy use of coal, which fuels the steel and chemical industries. Coal is also a source of household energy for some Belgians. Although Wallonia's high-grade coal has been used up, a few Flemish mines are still in operation. The yields in Kempenland are low, however, and the government heavily supports the industry.

Refineries in Antwerp allow Belgium to process imported crude oil, which meets about two-thirds of the nation's demand for petroleum.

A complex cloverleaf highway guides traffic through Namur province.

Transportation and Tourism

Belgium has a well-developed transportation network that includes railways, roads, and canals. Of the country's 80,000 miles of roads, more than 7,000 are international highways linked to major European cities. Paved roads connect the provinces, although in rural communities gravel routes are still common.

Belgium's first railway was built in 1835. The country now has one of Europe's most extensive rail networks, spanning more than 2,000 miles. The government-owned railroad connects all large Belgian cities and many small communities. A 35-mile underground rail system was completed in Brussels in the mid-1980s.

To move freight, Belgians use their country's many rivers and canals. These waterways bring raw materials to industrial sites and take finished goods to ports.

Antwerp, one of the world's largest ports, handles 85 percent of Belgian products shipped to foreign markets. Ghent is also a busy harbor, and Oostende and Zeebrugge are major ports for passenger ferries to and from Britain.

SABENA, Belgium's national airline, provides service to more than 50 countries. The airline's hub is in Brussels, and a second international airport is located near Antwerp. Smaller airfields exist near Oostende and Charleroi. Because Belgium is so small, domestic air traffic is light.

With its good transportation links, Belgium is easily accessible to tourists. Visitors are attracted by the country's wealth of art treasures and by centuries-old cities where ancient buildings have survived. Many travelers to Brussels stroll along the Grand Place, a large public square. The capital's Palace of Fine Arts and Museum

Cargo as well as passengers journey to distant cities on SABENA, the Belgian national airline.

Ancient banners flutter from one of the medieval guildhalls along the Grand Place. Restaurants, cafes, and historic buildings also line this central square in the capital.

Many tourists visit the battlefield monuments that reflect Belgium's stormy history. This U.S. tank is part of the display in Bastogne, the site of a long siege during World War II.

of Ancient Art contain a variety of works by famous Belgian painters.

Time seems to have passed by some parts of Brugge and Ghent, which maintain the appearance they had as great trading centers in the Middle Ages. Museums in Liège and Antwerp house some of the world's greatest art collections. In addition to beautiful forests, the Ardennes has numerous historic sites, many of which were the scenes of battles fought in ancient and modern times. The region also offers trails for hiking and limestone caves for exploration.

The Future

To some extent, the setting up of regional governments in the 1980s eased the serious economic friction between the Flemings and the Walloons. Nevertheless, the language differences show that there are still lingering conflicts in Belgian society and politics.

For the most part, however, Belgium in the early 1990s appeared to be solving

The imposing stock exchange in Brussels suggests Belgium's ongoing interest in international commerce.

The Flemish painter Quentin Massys created this scene of *The Money Changer and His Wife* **in the late fifteenth or early sixteenth century, when Belgian cities were centers of trade and banking.**

many of the problems it had experienced in the 1980s. Belgian firms were becoming more profitable, and the economy was growing. These improvements are likely to draw more foreign investment, which the country eagerly seeks.

Belgium's future is tied to that of western Europe. Economists believe that union among EC members will strengthen Europe's ability to compete in the large consumer markets of the United States and Japan. The outbreak of war in the Middle East in early 1991, however, reminded EC members that their union does not make them self-sufficient. The well-being of Belgium and its western European neighbors still depends on international trade and cooperation—goals that Belgium has long pursued.

Index